Los Boni̇...
in... ...ip
Douglas V. Steere
4.VII.71

MUTUAL
IRRADIATION

A
QUAKER
VIEW
OF
ECUMENISM

by

Douglas V. Steere

PENDLE HILL PAMPHLET 175

About the Author/Douglas Steere is the Thomas Wistar Professor of Philosophy, Emeritus, at Haverford College, and for the past six years has been chairman of the Friends World Committee. His books, nearly all of which deal with some phase of the life of contemplation and its relationship to the work of the world, have been widely read both in this country and in Britain.

The circumstances which led to the writing of the present pamphlet are given on the opposite page.

Requests for permission to quote or to translate should be addressed to Pendle Hill Publications, Wallingford, Pennsylvania 19086.

Copyright © January 1971 by Pendle Hill
Library of Congress catalog card number 73-146680

Printed in the United States of America by
Sowers Printing Company, Lebanon, Pennsylvania

January 1971: 7,500

Foreword

Douglas Steere has had a concern for what he calls "mutual irradiation" for almost two decades. On his first visit to India and Japan he and his wife, Dorothy, opened themselves to Hinduism and to Zen Buddhism, seeking to discern the message of each, and its relevance to the Christian life of the spirit. In the new climate created by their own vulnerability they discovered not only a deeper insight into the meaning of other religions, but a whole new level of understanding of their own traditions. "Mutual irradiation," even better than the term, "dialogue," described the process which had taken place.

This experience was further confirmed in an exposure to Islam in 1959, and found amazing extension in three sessions of Vatican Council II. In 1965 it led Douglas Steere to take part in drawing together a group of Roman Catholic and non-Catholic scholars to share with each other the treasures of their respective traditions, and to encourage one another in writing and providing guidance for the life of contemplation in the midst of the age in which we live. It also led in 1967 to carrying on two resident colloquia under the Friends World Committee; one in Japan, where ten Zen Buddhist masters and scholars met with their opposite numbers from the Christian community; the other in India, where a group of Hindu scholars and swamis experienced mutual irradiation with Christian scholars and men of the spirit.

It is against this background that Douglas Steere presented the Richard Cary Lecture of 1968 at the German Yearly Meeting in Bad Pyrmont. Delivered in German, it appears here for the first time in the English version in which it was originally

MONKS OF MT. TABOR

prepared. It makes no attempt to be an historical study of Quaker activities in ecumenism (which have now been admirably recorded by Ferner Nuhn). Rather, it reaches into the inner rationale of the ecumenical movement, and treats of those hesitations and roadblocks that Friends find surfacing as they develop intimate relationships, both within the Christian communion, and beyond it, in contact with members of the other great world religions. It searches the challenges and opportunities that lie immediately before us, and seeks to lay on Friends the responsibility of a possibly unique contribution to one of the most striking break-throughs that our century has produced.

THE EDITOR

Hans Denck, one of the German spiritual reformers of the 16th century, once said, "O my God how does it happen in this poor old world that thou art so great and yet nobody finds thee, that thou callest so loudly and yet nobody hears thee, that thou art so near and yet nobody feels thee, that thou givest thyself to everybody and yet nobody knows thy name. Men flee from thee and say they cannot find thee; they turn their backs and say they cannot see thee; they stop their ears and say they cannot hear thee" (*Vom Gesetz Gottes,* p. 27).

In the next century a French pilgrim of the spirit, Fénelon, adds "How few there are who are still enough to hear God speak." I do not believe that either the human perversity that Hans Denck refers to, or the want of inward stillness to which Fénelon points, can begin to exhaust the barriers that keep us from hearing what God has to say to us in the movements of our time and very especially in the ecumenical movement. Let us look behind some of these barriers and explore the content of that message. For if I do not mistake it, a message of importance for us is to be found in the ecumenical surge that has already taken place among the classical Protestants, the free churches, and the Orthodox within the World Council of Churches; and, since the Second Vatican Council, in the new gestures of openness between these groups and the Roman Catholic Church, itself; but especially in the new relations that are beginning to emerge between Christians and people from the other great religions of the world: Buddhists, Hindus, and Mus-

5

lims, whose members by far outnumber Christians in the share of the world's population which they include.

For those of us who suffer from hardening of the categories, the message to be found in this vast ecumenical movement will cause much pain. For those of us who may love to be tickled by the new, this message may well be a warning that it will not be as easy as it seems. But the painful and the difficult constitute the stuff of history. Arnold Toynbee, an English philosopher of history who interprets our crises as challenges that require a creative response, once said in my hearing that when the historians of a thousand years from now come to write the history of this century, they will be little interested in the minor domestic quarrels of communism and the so-called free-enterprise societies. What is likely to interest them most of all will be what happened in that superb challenge when for the first time in history, Buddhism and Christianity deeply interpenetrated each other; and he could have said as much for Hinduism and Islam.

If this new and far more extensive ecumenism is a challenge that is to prove a gift of God to us in this generation, it is well to note that as Kaethe Kollwitz once put it, "Every gift conceals a task." I propose to explore this gift and to try to see what small corner of the task has the Quaker name attached to it.

Ecumenism Means "World-Embracing"

You are all familiar with the literal definition of ecumenism which simply means "world-embracing", and is essentially spatial in its designation. But words seldom stop where they begin, and here in its implications, all kinds of overtones have to be added. Yet even these overtones begin from ecumenism's original meaning of overcoming barriers: barriers of fear, barriers of misunderstanding, barriers of irresponsibility for each

6

other. They also dip into ecumenism's original meaning by seeking to find what embraces them all; what common ground, if any, they may possess.

In the years immediately following the First World War, the Quakers worked in Poland distributing food and clothing. One of the workers who served a cluster of villages there became ill with typhus and in twenty-four hours he was dead. In this village there was only a Roman Catholic cemetery, and by canonical law it was quite impossible to bury one not of that confession in its consecrated ground. So they laid their cherished friend in a grave dug just outside the fence of the Roman Catholic cemetery. The next morning they discovered that in the night the villagers had moved the fence so that it embraced the grave.

This moving outwards of every type of fence so that it may embrace but not erase the unique and very special spiritual witness of the different religious groups, comes very close to the heart of what we really mean by the new ecumenism. We want to try to learn, even if with many painful mistakes along the way, how this creative interpenetration can be carried out in such a way that fences can be moved but at the same time the fresh unique witness of each group, actively operating in the whole, may be kept.

Four Postures of the Encounter of Religions

Christianity in its relations with the great world religions has four obvious alternatives. Its first relation could be that of attempting to collapse or to destroy the rival religion in the territory where it is working, or at least to be on hand with a good deal of satisfaction at its burial. The second is to merge with it in some form of syncretism. The third is a relationship of coexistence in which each religion agrees to honor the other and so respect its integrity that it will make no attempt whatever to challenge it or to seek to alter the allegiance of its members. The fourth is a relationship of what I would call "mutual irradiation" in which each is willing to expose itself with great openness to the inward message of the other, as well as to share its own experience, and to trust that whatever is the truth in each experience will irradiate and deepen the experience of the other.

This fourth approach is far from the wish to annihilate the other's religion or to merge with it in some new synthetic form of spiritual Esperanto. Nor is it the desire to remain in a state of hygienic coexistence, treating each religion as an aesthetic or cultural unity which must not in any way be intruded upon, as is the current temper among academic historians and anthropologists of religions. Rather, mutual irradiation would try to provide the most congenial setting possible for releasing the deepest witness that the Buddhist or Hindu or Muslim might make to his Christian companion, and that the Christian might in turn share with his non-Christian friend.

The fact of mutual irradiation is an existential one that goes beyond mere description and has to be experienced in order to be penetrated. It is not likely to leave any of the participants as they were when they started. But it may give some clue to the deeper dimension of what is meant by a truly ecumenical situation between the world religions.

To illustrate further this posture of mutual irradiation in the relationship of Christianity and the world religions it is important to see how these same four postures may be applied to the relationships that exist between the different confessions within Christianity. For while syncretism is less of a hazard, both the impulse to mutual extermination and the hygienic coexistence postures are everywhere apparent within the current Christian scene. Mutual irradiation appears only when we see ecumenism at its best moving from the wings toward the center of the stage.

"There, But for the Grace of God—"

Cardinal Cushing tells a story of his predecessor, during the depression in the '30's, visiting a miserably poor little parish outside Boston, Massachusetts, and asking the old priest how things were going. "Oh badly, very badly, your Eminence, but thank God they are going still worse for the Protestants!" And a Methodist tells of wiring his bishop for permission to bury a Baptist and receiving the reply "Permission granted. Bury as many Baptists as possible." But while we make these matters the target of humor, it is only fairly recently that we have begun to realize that what happens to one segment of a people's religion happens to all. If thousands of priests and nuns leave their posts and vocations we are all made poorer. Or if Protestant spiritual life is eaten away by the acids of affluence and urban secularism, the Roman Catholic Church in the area, far from profiting, will inevitably be impoverished.

It was moving to me as an American, who had followed Germany for the last four decades with more than an outward concern, to notice during the recent French and Algerian War the change of attitude which has taken place. France was in the agony of knowing that she must settle this conflict and give the Algerians their freedom, and yet at the same time not knowing how to manage it. Her old enemy, Germany, who in other periods would almost certainly have gloated over France's embarrassment, instead gave many evidences of feeling involved in the whole affair and, in a way, of suffering with France in her troubles. It seemed to me to be a witness to the ecumenical European mentality in Germany that had come out of the long suffering of the war and its aftermath.

Similarly, a true ecumenism creates a situation where each religious group feels concern for the outcome of its fellow religionist's situation and can rejoice and find itself enriched when it produces an unmistakable saint, or a groundswell of holiness, and can feel as equally involved in its misfortunes and say, not "There but for the grace of God go I," but rather, "There go I."

As for coexistence within Christianity, all but the darkest corners of the Christian scene are moving to acknowledge it today. Even in the Latin regions, where the Roman Catholic Church has resisted coexistence for so long, the Second Vatican Council's acknowledgment of religious liberty has helped the Roman Catholic authorities in countries like Italy, Spain, and Portugal to see this less as the disaster which the fearful wing of the Spanish bishops predicted during the Council, and more as the beginning of a discovery of some common ground.

But coexistence is at best only a transitional state. For when this common ground begins to be cultivated, there can be no remaining in a state of fenced-off isolation. Then the alternative becomes either to drop back into the earlier defensive positions or to move out into a condition of interpenetration and of common undertakings and seeing what the common ground requires of each.

This existential situation is what is really meant by true ecumenism, and we must now turn to see more clearly what it might involve, and if we as Quakers should decide to participate in it, what treasures we might have to bring to it and what might come to us out of our active involvement in it.

Quaker Hesitations Before the Ecumenical Movement

Historically, Quakers have approached the Protestant ecumenical negotiations of the last half century with pronounced hesitation. To be sure, we, like every group, have had our "ecumaniacs" who always look wistfully at every religion as better than their own. We have also had our serious Quaker ecumenists who from the earilest days of the Church Unity

10

meetings in Lausanne have shared faithfully in the progressive stages of the ecumenical movement that led to the formation of the World Council of Churches in 1948. A large part of our American Quaker membership is at present officially represented in that body.

At our best, we as Friends have touched a spring of life that reaches beyond forms. William Penn and John Woolman have testified to our unity. William Penn once declared "The humble, meek, merciful, just, pious, and devout souls of the world are everywhere of one religion; and when death has taken off the mask, they will know one another, though the divers liveries they wear here makes them strangers." (*Some Fruits of Solitude,* Pt. 1, No. 519). Two generations later, John Woolman out of his inward experience of tendering was able to write, "There is a principle which is pure, placed in the human mind, which in different places and in different ages hath had different names. It is, however, pure and proceeds from God. It is deep and inward, confined to no forms of religion nor excluded from any, where the heart stands in perfect sincerity. In whomsoever this takes root and grows, of what nation soever they become brethren in the best sense of the expression." ("Considerations on the Keeping of Negroes," *Works,* 1774, p. 325).

From the outset of the Ecumenical Movement Friends, who believed in peaceful conflict resolution, were glad to see badly splintered Protestantism mending its differences. They also rejoiced in the meetings of the *Life and Work* section which sought to mobilize the Protestant concern for the great social issues of our time. But Friends found themselves in a situation that was essentially foreign to their mind and experience in the all-important *Faith and Order* section's interminable efforts, in session after session, to produce a creedal statement of Christian belief that all would find agreeable, or to find some formula that would satisfy all present on the matter of church government: the role of the bishop, the status of the presbyters, the

11

validity of orders, mixed communion and the rest. Always there was a suspicion that in these theological and institutional attempts to storm the barricades, they were coming at the matter from the wrong angle. British Friends were blunt and refused outright to submit to the creedal formula that was required for membership in the World Council of Churches, even though they had been among the founding members of the British Council of Churches and have consistently sent theologically trained members like H. G. Wood and Maurice Creasey to serve as participating observers at the W. C. C. sessions.

Quakers and the Third Stream

Continental and Scandinavian Friends, as I know them, are made up very largely of those who have come away from both the Protestant and the Roman Catholic streams and have fiercely prized the close fellowship and the theological and institutional freedom which they have found in the Society of Friends. Although they may not have formulated it precisely, many feel themselves part of something that is a third force— that is neither Roman Catholic nor Protestant but part of the Christian mystical stream that has nurtured them all. This stream might one day draw all back into its current, immersing them in a new dimension of concern for their fellows that would renew the life of both West and East.

Because of such reservations there has always seemed to me to be an essential conflict or antinomy in Quakers' minds about their own intimate involvement in the Protestant coalition which, in spite of the Orthodox connection, until recently gave the dominant color to the World Council of Churches. On the one hand was their own more inward approach where, in their Quaker meetings, they experienced the mystical stream in which institutional and ceremonial and theological differences receded.

Here they felt experientially, as Penn and Woolman have indicated, the basic oneness of those who know the costly love that is poured out upon them as they feel "joined to all the living." This approach made them want to be a part of anything that would heal even a little of the torn and divided body of the Christian world. It made them want to attend these ecumenical gatherings, and to share in the deep experiences of worship and fellowship and joint responsibility for peace and social concern that emerged.

On the other hand, there have always been two aspects of the Quaker reluctance to full-scale participation. Conscious of living in a third order which was neither Catholic nor Protestant, many Friends were hesitant to become inextricably identified with the essentially Protestant segment while the greater breach, namely, that between the Protestant and the Roman Catholic, and the Roman Catholic and the Orthodox, still existed.

A Slumbering Revolutionary Ferment in the Quakers

In the second place, it should not be overlooked that there is always a slumbering revolutionary element in the Quakers which distrusts ecclesiastical structures of all sorts, and suspects that Christ's radical message may well have become a victim of the "Constantinian conspiracy" to which nearly all of the established churches adhere in one form or another. This element of Quakerism regards itself as a *movement* rather than a church; it profoundly suspects that no coalitions of institutions, church governments, or theologies or no religious conglomerates can restore the inward liberty which they have at moments tasted and known in this Quaker fellowship and that they covet for all men. Therefore, to enter the ecumenical association as just another small and insignificant ecclesiastical body and to participate in it as such, would be to rob them of their revolutionary status, and would involve an acknowledgment of themselves as just one more formal religious organization.

This second area of reluctance has in it a certain strain of denominational egotism—an egotism in regard to its own unique and irreplaceable genius which every religious body that has ventured into one of these ecumenical undertakings has had to come to terms with. But in the case of the Quakers, its source may be untameably radical, and may not be unconnected with their corporate experience of the Christian mystical stream.

The events of the five years have been drastic enough, however, to compel Friends to make a thorough re-examination of the negative side of this antinomy. For John XXIII and his Second Vatican Council have gone a long way in changing the climate and in setting in motion whole new levels of Roman Catholic communication and understanding with both the Protestants and the Orthodox. John XXIII also expressed a vision that does not leave even the second aspect of this negative side of the Quaker antinomy untouched when he hinted at the revolutionary consequence of accenting the universality of God's love as expressed in the type-man Jesus Christ, a love, incidentally, that the Gospel of John can only express as "For God so loved *the world.*"

The Fourth Gospel does not say "For God so loved the Church," nor that "God so loved all Christians," but that "God so loved *the world.*" Here the floodgates are opened to all the world: to those in other world religions and even to unbelievers, to those in what Paul Tillich used to call the "latent" church as against the "patent" or visible church. Of this "holy invisible church," the French Roman Catholic novelist, Georges Bernanos, writes in one of his last essays, "The holy invisible church which we know includes pagans, heretics, schismatics and non-believers whom God alone knows . . . the communion of Saints . . . which of us is sure of belonging to it?" (*Last Essays,* Trans. Joan and Barry Ulanov, Greenwood Press: Westport, Conn., 1968, pp. 235-6).

Here implied in John XXIII's vision is a concept radical enough to challenge any revolutionary. The implications of this vision in regard to religious structures are as mysteriously open as could be expressed, and their practical applications cry out for implementation.

Yet in all of this vision there is not only an outflanking of the negative reservations but basically an accent on the positive side that draws us almost irresistibly to join ecumenically with our brothers in sharing both our gifts and our tasks. This accent is John XXIII's calling us to witness to the operative presence, here and now, of this fathomless love and concern that is at the heart of things: a presence which is already actively at work in the unconscious life of every part of the creation. By more contemplation, more piercing communication and sharing, more costly common undertakings of social concern, we might help to emerge above the threshold of the world's consciousness.

It may be one of God's ironies that the Quakers should receive this amazing articulation from an interim Pope in the third quarter of the 20th century. But stranger things than this have happened, and it would be hard to find a more moving appeal to our own intimate experience of this supporting mystical stream that has been flowing always through the unconscious life of all men everywhere but that broke out into history in the life of Jesus Christ and has gone on moving like an underground river that lifts the water table in us all.

Functional Ecumenism

My own notion of the current implementing of this vision is a functional ecumenism that begins with all of us encouraging each other to practice our own religious tradition to the hilt and to share our experiences with each other in every creative way we can devise. It does not propose any monolithic merging or any wholesale syncretism, and the fear that many have that we shall be swept into unacceptable structures and creeds seems to

15

me to be quite unfounded. It also assumes as its ground rule that we shall not seek to detach each other's members to swell our own numbers, although occasional transfers may take place. These need not be regarded as ecumenical casualties but rather be generously accepted on both sides. We should also be prepared to join with other confessions in all kinds of common explorations and common tasks.

A truly functional ecumenism wants to witness to the world how much God cares, and if this means stopping a war; or trying to learn how to share more equitably the world's material resources; or meeting an emergency human need, or joining the poor; or sending brotherly teachers and companions to live and share with those in another area; or teaching one another how to meditate, or how to pray, or how to kindle corporate adoration, or how to grow in the life of devotion, or how to use the lives of past saints and heroes to re-kindle our commitment; or how great art, painting, sculpture and music can expand the soul; or how personal guidance and therapy may release the deeper life in us; or how the world of plants and animals and water and wind can temper our souls; a functional ecumenism will open us in these and in other areas to the witness of our fellows, whether Christian or the adherents of other world religions.

A Zen Buddhist-Christian Colloquium

Let me give an example of this functional ecumenism at work in a recent colloquium for which the Quakers took the initiative. In the spring of 1967, under the auspices of the Friends World Committee, the Quakers invited a small group of Zen Buddhists and Christians to meet together. In the group were ten leading Zen Buddhist personalities, one of whom was a woman. Both the Rinzai and Soto persuasions were represented within the group. Ten Christian scholars were also invited, four of whom

16

were members of Roman Catholic orders: two Jesuits, a Dominican, and a Carmelite, together with five Protestants and a Japanese Quaker professor as the chairman.

There was a small Quaker team present which included a Japanese and an American woman. They took little part in the discussion, which was, by the way, conducted in Japanese, but served as hosts and tried to help create an atmosphere of friendly openness in which a free exchange between members of this group could take place.

The gathering involved living together for five days in a beautiful isolated spot by the sea at Oiso, some two hours by train from Tokyo. We were favored by having a Japanese villa entirely at our disposal for the meetings. No academic papers were given because no one needed to be impressed and the members were quite able to speak without notes! The morning discussions centered in turn upon one of the two stated topics: "The Inward Journey" and "Social Responsibility for the Ordering of Our World."

Each participant had an opportunity to give an opening talk and there was ample time for continuing the issues raised, for questioning each other, and for sharing both the insights and the failures of our personal and corporate efforts in different areas. From the outset, the discussion was highly personal, disarmingly frank, and intensely moving. All of the afternoons were left free for resting or walking or visiting, and the evenings were mostly given to some sharing of Zen art or Christian music.

Japanese Christian scholars in the course of the exchange began to discover that they, like nearly all Japanese Christians who have come to Christianity from Buddhism, have a layer of traditional Buddhism in their unconscious which they have largely sealed over, perhaps so that it would not threaten their Christian commitment. It became increasingly clear to them as they talked that an interior dialogue had long been going on in their unconscious and that this liberating occasion enabled them

17

to bring this hidden dialogue out into the open and to re-assess what of their Buddhist past, instead of being fearfully excluded, might be thankfully accepted and utilized to their great enrichment.

The Zen Buddhists, in turn, had nearly all encountered the figure of Jesus Christ at some stage in their pilgrimage. They followed carefully and responded most sensitively to the Christians' witness, especially to their responsibility for peace and poverty, but also to their experiences of the inward journey, the inward crises, and the life of prayer and renewal.

Quakers and Zen Buddhists

The question has often been raised as to why the Quakers should have chosen this small élite group, the Zen Buddhists, as the first world religion with which to conduct such an exchange. Our choice could be justified on cultural grounds, because this group, although small in number, occupy a unique place in Japan, and are in many ways a living and highly articulate organ of the inward, non-Western spiritual Japanese life. They are, as well, a group who may one day take a guiding role in re-kindling this spirit when the momentary Japanese immersion in Western secularism has run its course. But sound as I believe these reasons for our choice to have been, it must also be confessed that Quakers found this a natural group to turn to, since for some time we have been in the most friendly relations with the Zen Buddhists who as anti-liturgical, iconoclastic, unconventional witnesses to the spirit rather than the letter of the law have, in the Buddhist world, some marked similarities to Quakers in the Christian community.

The Zen flavor of these common traits comes through best of all in their innumerable stories. Two Zen monks were forced to spend a bitterly cold night in a Buddhist temple. One monk takes a wooden statue of the Buddha and chops it up for wood to make a fire, assuring the other monk that the Buddha would strongly approve of this action! Two Zen monks meet a beautiful girl at a river crossing. She dared not cross because of the powerful current. One monk put her on his shoulder, Christopher-like, and carried her across. The two monks walked on in silence until late in the afternoon when one of them blurted out his accusation. "You broke the law of our Order this morning. You touched a woman." To which the other monk answered quietly, "Are you still carrying that girl? I set her down on the river bank early this morning."

The Zen Professor Hisamatsu, when he was in Cambridge, Massachusetts, several years ago, was reproached for refusing a cocktail in a Harvard Professor's apartment. He politely turned the question of why he did not drink spirits into inquiring of the surprised Harvard Professor why he *did* drink them. When his Western colleague replied that they took the edge off and made his consciousness a little blurred, Professor Hisamatsu observed that these were exactly the reasons why he abstained.

Mutual Irradiation Searches Quakers

With so many characteristics that were congenial to Friends, it was a really challenging shock to find the fierce and unyielding priority which the Zen in our meetings gave, in these conversations, to what they call "going into the mountain"—the Zen term for turning inward in meditation and searching relentlessly to find the inward Buddhahood or the new angle of vision before anything else is done. When we were told of a Zen master who rebuked a novice for helping a man push his cart, insisting that he get back to his real work, we blinked. Quakers, too, believe that a clean act must come from the inside out like a rose-bud unfolding, and not the way we make a box. We, too, believe in the turning inward to find the true ground for any valid concern. But we have experienced often that "the mountain" where we meet another's need, may open the way to the inward "mountains," and we found ourselves so much less sure than our guests, the Zen masters, that "going into the mountain," as they know it, necessarily comes first.

How this discussion searched us all! Even today the consciousness of what our Zen Buddhist friends would say to this and many other issues rises in the parliament of my mind that is seeking to decide an issue. I now carry within me my companions' experience and witness, and it often inwardly queries my own! The willingness of these Zen Buddhists to pay any price for this inward breakthrough, and after its occurrence, to help prepare others to find the new angle of vision for themselves, searched not only the Quakers but all the Christians present. It illustrates true ecumenism carrying out its irradiative function.

The way the Zen Buddhists openly acknowledge the presence of the body, and their use of posture and breathing to open them to greater inner concentration, was accentuated by the testimony of a Jesuit that his own use of this Zen practice had restored his Christian life of prayer, grown dry and dead after many years of Ignatian meditation techniques. The Zen use not only of posture and breathing but of diet, of long vigils of meditation, of hard manual work, of close spiritual direction under a Zen master, all indicated their utter seriousness in getting at the pearl of great price, and probed the rocking chair attitude of so much of Christian practice.

The Zen humor about themselves and their professions, their adaptability, and their resiliently sensible minds were not lost on us. Nor did the humble, open way the Christians confessed both their efforts and their failures, fail to move the Zen Buddists, as evidenced by their questions and the long personal visits in the afternoon periods. The Christians admitted the difficulty they had in carrying out their social testimonies; in their use of the Bible to challenge and judge their lives; in their experience of prayer, and of finding the continual confrontation of the figure of Jesus Christ in shaping their lives. The informal and free visitation of one another's periods of corporate exercise was a further evidence of this openness.

When in the 1890's, Gilbert Bowles, the American Quaker apostle to Japan, arrived in that country, he declared, "Every man shall be my teacher." In this colloquium in Japan I think that there was hardly a participant who did not experience something of this mood of openness, for both by day and by night, we truly listened to each other.

A Roman Catholic lay orientalist scholar, Dr. Jacques Cuttat (who had been for five years the Swiss Ambassador to India), in a striking manuscript which he submitted in 1964 to the newly established Vatican Secretariat for the Non-Christian Religions, urged Christians to learn to listen to what the Holy Spirit has to say to us through the faith in Hinduism and Buddhism and Islam. He lays down as a requirement for significant dialogue that each must give to the other's faith the amplitude of love, postpone the value judgment, and "suspend for a time our explicit adhesion to our own religious communion in order to understand the non-Christian brother as he understands himself." He follows this by the concomitant condition that the listener in turn make his witness to his own experience. When this takes place, Cuttat adds, "We have what can be called a truly religious 'inter-religious space'. In such a space God's spirit can blow as it wills, breathe where He wills." (Manuscript to Secretariat for Non-Christian Religions, 1964, p. 6) Our experience as the Quaker hosts of this Japanese gathering was that these words were not rhetoric but that they expressed with amazing precision what happened in our midst. It is certainly no exaggeration to say that such genuine opening of the inward doors to each other is so rare and wonderful that it needs to be repeated often and on all levels.

In the course of this colloquium we had many confirmations of the difference that it made to have, not just Quakers or Protestants or Roman Catholics, but almost the whole Christian spectrum represented, and it must be said that they complemented each other excellently. It made a different situation for our Zen participants, too, to know that they faced an ecumenical Christian group. On the Zen side to have both the Rinzai and the Soto members present, supplementing each other, also gave a deeper cast to their witness.

A Hindu-Christian Colloquium

In the month of April 1967, the Friends World Committee was host to a similar gathering, this time of Hindu and Christian scholars who were ecumenically chosen and made up of three Roman Catholics, one Syrian Orthodox, one Mar Thoma Bishop, four Protestants, and an Indian Quaker educator as Chairman. We lived together for a full week at Ootacamund in the South of India. Again the intimate process of mutual irradiation performed its miracle.

From the very outset of this meeting, there was a deep sense that we met in a season where our own and the world's spiritual need was acute. In his opening remarks, Father Klaus Klostermaier, a German Catholic monk, expressed the stake that we all have in the vast spiritual capital of God-expectancy which Hinduism has created in the hearts of the common people of India. "I think that Indians should know that the highly secularized West has a deep appreciation for the amount of spiritual life that is still present in the common people of India. If this spiritual substance of India should be lost by influences in India today which tend to depreciate it or rub it out, the whole world would be the loser. We must help each other, we Christians and Hindus, to preserve this precious tradition in India. Hindus and Christians here in India may influence the whole world so that

22

this colloquium, should it fail, would fail mankind at a critical point in the world."

The well-known English Benedictine monk, Bede Griffiths, who was another of the Christian scholars present at Ootacamund, underlined this desperate sense of common need. "I feel the intense importance of this meeting of the long tradition of prayer and contemplation that has marked Europe with that of the Indian tradition of contemplation. The West stands in danger of neglecting the life of contemplation and it is important for it to have contact with the revitalized life of contemplation in Hinduism which some of the 19th and 20th century figures like Ramakrishna and Vivekhananda have done so much to further."

The same fear of a fracture in this capacity for inner awareness in modern man had already been stated in an impassioned plea to the Japanese colloquium that came from the above mentioned Professor Hisamatsu, who is perhaps Zen Buddhism's greatest living interpreter, and who was prevented by serious illness from sharing in the colloquium as he had intended. In a message to the colloquium he said: "All we human beings are now threatened by the crisis, the split in subjectivity, its confusion and its loss. To reverse this crisis and to . . . realize a stable post-modern original subjectivity, this is a universal and vital task" and he laid on the members of the colloquium an urgent need for their "ceaseless effort for the solution of the problem."

These men and women who were taking part in this tiny but intense ecumenical experience of mutual irradiation were welded together by their acute sense of need, confirming the wisdom of the promise that "not in your *skill* but in your *need* will you be blessed."

Vicarious Participation in Dialogue

It is obvious that only a few can participate in gatherings of this kind, but happily a whole new literature is now giving us a vicarious sharing in the religious insights of these great world religions, and there is almost no European country today where some direct access may not be had to practicing members of the great world religions. To read the Norwegian Pastor Reichelt's moving books on Buddhism, or Father H. M. Enomiya-Lassalle's *Zen Buddhismus* or *Zen: the Way to Enlightenment,* (Taplinger Publishing Co.: N.Y., 1968) is to feel the Zen message of the devaluation of the transitory; to sense the meaning of its focus on the opening of the lens of inward awareness; to wonder at its reverence for all life—plants, animals, men—in its principle of non-injury; and to be stirred by its Bodhisattvas who lay aside the bliss of Nirvana in order to spend themselves in helping others in moving toward this goal.

This universal invitation to a vast introversion which may loosen man's greed and his acquisitive clutching at the world of nature and of his fellows, and by loosening his ego-centric pretension may permit him to share whole new dimensions of awareness—this is a principal work of the Buddhist world.

The Bhagavad Gita, the New Testament-like parables and stories of the 19th century Ramakrishna, and the philosophical writings of the 20th century Aurobindo are all grist for the mill to those who would try to feel into the world of Hinduism. Hinduism, too, is marked by this same inward-turning accent. It invites all men to discover that their self-obsessed souls are in reality conjunct with the soul of the infinite Godhead itself and that the peace of Samadhi comes with an overwhelming realization of this oneness. India's age-long skills in leading men to this discovery are a part of the world's treasury, and Dr. Jacques Cuttat says of them, in his manuscript to the Vatican

24

Secretariat (p. 15) "The great 'lesson' of the spiritual East is not universality, it is spiritual concentration." And this concentration for him means a highly developed skill in resisting the soul's natural tendency to dispersion. In *Encounter of Religions* he writes, "The more consciousness grows deep and centered (that is to say detached from the ego) the more it becomes permeable to the presence of the transcendent Divinity" (Desclee: N. Y. 1960, p. 37). In the same volume Cuttat also notes that Eastern spirituality transfers the primacy in the spiritual order from speculation to practice and that it insists that this aspiration to the Divine is a normal one, normal not in the sense of frequent or easy, but of being inherent in the human vocation, as opposed to "spiritual luxury" (p. 38).

This possibility of realizing what great common spring and source of life and being is concealed in the separate souls of all men has produced over the centuries a sense of God-expectancy among the common people of India and makes them look for God to come disguised in any stranger that may appear. One evening Vinoba Bhave, the great Hindu follower of Gandhi, when he had spent the whole day interviewing two thousand villagers, was asked whether he was not feeling tired. He replied "I have been visited by God over two thousand times today." (Bede Griffiths, *Christian Ashram*, Darton Longman Todd, London, 1966, p. 122) This God-expectancy has led simple village Hindus to welcome the stranger, to seek his darshan and his blessing that may perhaps lead to God's breaking through in his own bosom.

Hindu culture has given to the plain and elementary things a dignity and has even brought to its followers a contentment with what Woolman calls "a life so simple that a little suffices." Hinduism's stages of life have made the later years of life a time not of boredom and an incessant search for diversion but a very special time for the healing of the soul, and has taught its people that the most holy ones of every generation who keep

25

the fire alive for us all are not likely to be found in great religious organizations but hidden away in unexpected places and one may come upon them anywhere.

To meet Islam in Kenneth Cragg's fine books, *The Call of the Minaret, Sandals at the Mosque,* and *The Dome and the Rock,* is to know instantly that you are in the prophetic Semitic world again and that now the way is less the way of inwardness than the strait path of obedience. Here a fierce monotheism appears, but it is a monotheism of a transcendent God who nevertheless cares infinitely for his people and singles out each one for his special concern. Islam witnesses to what it means to live in the Providence of God. A devout Muslim feels that his goods, his family, his very life itself are all at the disposal of Allah, the All Merciful and the All Just. To take what comes as if from the hands of Allah, and to discover what message for me is written in this event—this is "self-abandonment to Divine Providence" which Islam calls for.

The five spoken daily prayers are reminders of the all watchful presence of Allah, and like a Quaker meeting for worship, they require no consecrated building but can be accomplished anywhere. Clarence Pickett, in the early days of the United Nations, when no meditation room was available, once reported finding Sir Zaphrilla Khan, then the Pakistani delegate, with his feet sticking out of a U.N. lobby telephone booth quietly absorbed in saying his prayers at the appointed time!

Ramadan, the month of fasting during the light of day, is again a reminder of Who has the whole world in his hands. To see the Muslim family loyalty and the offices of hospitality that have been built upon this structure is again to be probed and irradiated in such a way that one's Christian profession is profoundly stirred. More than one dormant Christian has, like Charles de Foucauld, been called back to his own faith by seeing the fierce devotion to the Divine Providence practiced so unflinchingly by the Muslims among whom he had lived.

These flashes of a few of the traits that mark the world religions are only hints, but they point to the temper of receptivity, to the temper of asking continually "what is the Holy Spirit saying to me as a Christian, as a Quaker, in the witness of this other religion?" This is the attitude which marks the truly ecumenical approach.

"Every Gift Conceals a Task"

This kind of daring ecumenical approach requires a climate of confidence that is highly exacting and that will make costly demands of us on the devotional, intellectual and institutional level and perhaps in just that order.

I believe that Quakers do have a small but a peculiarly important role to play as catalysts in the kind of ecumenical hospitality that has been suggested here. This hospitality is not only between Christians and those of the great world religions but equally among the Christian confessions themselves. I doubt if there is a neighborhood where, with some initiative, concerned Friends could not find a way to make some unique contribution.

At their best, I think that Friends are naturally oriented to start at the right end of this ecumenical endeavor—namely to begin from within and to draw the whole ecumenical process in this direction. Their life and witness to the interior religion, which puts a minimal accent on outer forms, makes them at home with widely diverse groups. Yet their inward sense of being joined both to Him and to all the living, means a witness against violence and for the unlimited liability that we owe to each other. Again this authenticates the inward witness and cuts across all kinds of divisions.

Marius Grout, a French Quaker who died some 20 years ago, once put very starkly this norm for the inward and the outward in Quaker experience. "If contemplation which introduces us to

27

the very heart of creation does not inflame us with such a love that it gives us, together with deep joy, the understanding of the infinite misery of the world, it is a vain kind of contemplation, it is the contemplation of a false God. The sign of true contemplation is charity. By your capacity for forgiveness shall I recognize your God and also your opening your arms to all creation." ("On Contemplation," *Friends World News,* London #16, 1945, p. 1).

It is because a few Friends in every generation have truly lived in this spirit and have given us this expectation and this encouragement, that we are able to approach Buddhists and Hindus, as we have done recently and to find them trusting and open to join us. It is because our fellow Christians find in this tradition of ours something authentic that they join with us in such colloquia and let us put our questions concerning the outer sacraments and existing Christian institutional structures in the intra-Christian meetings.

But both this Quaker tradition and the ecumenical task to which it draws us make demands upon us before which we may well quiver. For how well we know that instead of being the seasoned veterans of the inward life that others assume we are, we so often live in inward mediocrity if not in poverty. A Zen Buddhist master asked a Quaker how he found it possible to counter the dispersive forces of life in the midst of our secular world and to keep attentive in the inward center by devoting to it only a single hour every seven days. It is a fair question. A Hindu staying in a Western home for a month finally asked his host, "When is the time that you take for the healing of the soul?" It, too, is a fair question. These very questions to us are a part of God's gift to us in the ecumenical movement. For they send us back to our own group knowing that we cannot remain as we are and meet the need that is before us. There is no alternative to being brought back into the seat of yielding and of tendering again and again and again.

The Intellectual Task

On the intellectual side it is doubtful if Friends are likely to make any decisive contribution to this deeper ecumenism. We have never abounded in theologically oriented members and our whole tradition has tended to give to this area a low priority. What then have Friends to say to Teilhard de Chardin when he puts his challenge to the Christian world of our day as to whether Jesus Christ was not really a provincial and that our world may well have superceded him? In *The Divine Milieu,* he asks "Is the Christ of the Gospels imagined and loved within the dimensions of the Mediterranean world capable of still embracing and still forming the center of our prodigiously expanded universe? Is the world not in the process of becoming more vast, more close, more dazzling than Jehovah? Will it not twist our religion asunder, eclipse our God?" (*The Divine Milieu,* Harper & Row: N. Y., 1960, p. 4)

Our only reply might be that having felt inwardly in the presence of the living Christ both the joy and the misery of the world and having felt our arms being opened to the whole creation, while we may not ourselves at this point be able adequately to formulate a view of the universal Christ, we can be among those who are most open to it. For this universal burst of the limitless love of God has brought us not only to a Jesus Christ who is a "man for others," but to one who is "a man for all others," and to sense that his very uniqueness is grounded in his universality.

Feeling this openness may for Friends be accompanied by a somewhat unique fearlessness in entering these ecumenical engagements in confidence that they will not rob us of Jesus Christ. The small clues that we have had up to now would indicate that any truth that we have found in these great world religions has only sharpened the urgency of Christ's inward call upon us and has given us a new sense of how little we yet know of him, and of how much we have yet to learn perhaps through these very meetings with our brothers in other Christian faiths and in the world religions. What these encounters do rob us of is the picture of Jesus Christ in our conventional Western institutional and theological dress. And what they have lavished upon us is that he would have infinitely more to disclose to us, if our free responses both to him and to each other were more adequate.

The intellectual implications of the universal in this haunting figure of Christ are still almost unexplored by Christian thought. What fresh insights into man's inmost being may await us if and when the prophetic type of religion that accentuates the personal responsible core of a man can meet the profound Buddhist and Hindu concentration upon dimensions of consciousness and awareness, in which the "myself" seems to be transcended.

The Quaker contribution to the institutional implications of such ecumenical interpenetration may seem to be modest. The very sight of an intimate fellowship of lay Christians, whose own structural requirements are both minimal and flexible, but who nevertheless take seriously the priesthood of all believers and the maximal participation of all involved may have its uses. Certainly from the Quaker side, such encounters make for a fresh appreciation of the wide variety of institutional postures that mark both the Christian and the non-Christian communities. They may broaden Quaker horizons, produce in us a salutary humility, and bring a realization that the stream of God's mercy can flow down through more than one shape of institutional river-bed. It may also remind Quakers that unless their own members are truly "in the life," even our own modest structures can become highly burdensome. In our ordering of our own affairs, what is sometimes called "Quaker patience" in arriving at a decision can by less charitable lips be spoken of as "decision by exhaustion."

Indifference and "Rucksichtlosigkeit"*

Now in all of this exploration of the gifts and the tasks of such an ecumenical approach, there should be no minimizing of the need for a climate of sincere seeking, for "with an insincere man God can do nothing." And this climate of sincere seeking needs to be clearly distinguished from that which might be called a climate of indifference. Among the latter is the insistence that since man knows so little of the ultimate mystery, the ways by which he 'races his camel to the next mirage' are essentially inconsequential. Another is the climate of an indulgent, euphoric optimism that assumes that it makes little difference which road you travel since "all roads up the mountain lead to the same summit."

I once asked Martin Buber what was the secret of those amazing conversations that used to take place in the '30's in that famous little Frankfurt group in which the Quakers, Rudolf Schlosser and Alfons Paquet, took an active part. He thought for a time and then almost shouted out a single word in answer to my question: "Rucksichtlosigkeit." For the ecumenical encounter to be creative, there is required not only the tender effort to understand, but an equally frank and open climate that acknowledges that genuine differences exist and that they matter, in fact matter terribly; and it will encourage each to probe his differences and to share them in all of their starkness. But it has found, and may find increasingly, that something happens in the course of understanding another's truth that irradiates and lights up one's own tradition and that on rare occasions may even give one a hint of a truth that embraces both, a hint of a hidden convergence.

---

* Ruthless frankness in pressing the argument to its furthest conclusion.

If we should regard the great world religions as a row of summits in a common chain of mountains we might be able to counter the proverb that "mountains never meet" by the observation that "men do meet," and that when they do meet, on the deepest level, they confirm in each other the deepest things that each knows, and lift for each other a further curtain into the ultimate truth.